WONDER VERSE

A Collection Of Creativity

Edited By Lynsey Evans

First published in Great Britain in 2025 by:

YoungWriters Est. 1991

Young Writers
Remus House
Coltsfoot Drive
Peterborough
PE2 9BF
Telephone: 01733 890066
Website: www.youngwriters.co.uk

All Rights Reserved
Book Design by Ashley Janson
© Copyright Contributors 2024
Softback ISBN 978-1-83685-193-6
Printed and bound in the UK by BookPrintingUK
Website: www.bookprintinguk.com
YB0626L

FOREWORD

WELCOME READER,

For Young Writers' latest competition *Wonderverse*, we asked primary school pupils to explore their creativity and write a poem on any topic that inspired them. They rose to the challenge magnificently with some going even further and writing stories too! The result is this fantastic collection of writing in a variety of styles.

Here at Young Writers our aim is to encourage creativity in children and to inspire a love of the written word, so it's great to get such an amazing response, with some absolutely fantastic pieces. This open theme of this competition allowed them to write freely about something they are interested in, which we know helps to engage kids and get them writing. Within these pages you'll find a variety of topics, from hopes, fears and dreams, to favourite things and worlds of imagination. The result is a collection of brilliant writing that showcases the creativity and writing ability of the next generation.

I'd like to congratulate all the young writers in this anthology, I hope this inspires them to continue with their creative writing.

CONTENTS

Abbey Gate College, Saighton

Nerea Morente (9)	1

Albyn School, Aberdeen

Aurélien Desindes (8)	2
Magnus Foy (10)	3

Amesbury CE Primary School, Amesbury

Connie Gregson (10)	4
Ottilie Gregson (7)	5

Aspin Park Community Primary, Knaresborough

Matthew Craddock (10)	6
Morgan Hamilton (10)	7

Belhaven Hill School, Dunbar

Sophia Diamond (10)	8
Alice Lindsay (11)	10
Holly Hutchison (10)	11

Bolton Parish Church CE Primary School, Bolton

Maira Usman (10)	12

Bonneygrove Primary School, Cheshunt

Naimah Hussain (10)	13
Joshua Kimani (9)	14
Lexi Khan-Vigus (10)	16
Adam Chaudhry (9)	18
Noah Michael (10)	20
Grace McMullins (10)	21
Jake Timson (9)	22
Sydney Spink (9)	23
Elif Michalski (9)	24
Lily-Mae Catlin (9)	25
Olivia Walsh (8)	26
Alex Harling (9)	27
Sophie Schuster (9)	28
Millie Brown (9)	29
Mira Ustun (9)	30
Orlagh Peet (9)	31
Dino Pacitti (9)	32
Hope Mcglynn (9)	33
Libby Doughty (9)	34
Kacper Zuk (9)	35
Charlie Bickenstaff (9)	36

Brindishe Green Primary School, Hither Green

Roshan Govind (9)	37

Bryngwran Primary School, Bryngwran

Deio Earnshaw (11)	39

Carswell Community Primary School, Abingdon

Mansaha Seidu (8)	40
Maisie Tutty (8)	41

Copthorne Preparatory School, Copthorne

Aidan Skelton (11)	42
Sophia Berkovic (11)	43
Anastasia Glover (9)	44

Countess Gytha Primary School, Queen Camel

Aurelia Pullen (9)	45

Dalton School, Dalton

Grace Long (10)	46

Dean Field Community Primary School, Ovenden

Jessica Stevenson (10)	47

Dixons Allerton Academy, Allerton

Maheen Shamoon (11)	48
Hiba Javed (10)	49

Downpatrick Primary School, Downpatrick

Sophie MCDonnell (9)	50
Katherine Napier (10)	51

English Bicknor CE (VC) Primary School, English Bicknor

Tara Hawker (7)	52

Featherstone All Saints CofE Academy, North Featherstone

Max Slater (11)	53

Flax Hill Junior Academy, Gillway

Aurora McMahon (10)	54

Gawthorpe Community Academy, Gawthorpe

Zoey Broadfield (9)	55

Greatwood Community Primary And Nursery School, Skipton

Meredith Reffin (8)	56

Halyrude Primary School, Peebles

Liza Kruchinina (10)	57
Maria O'Hara (11)	58
Sadie Noble (11)	60
Ellie McCubbing (11)	62
Gosia Czuprynko (10)	63
Jula Sidorjakova (10)	64
Casey Morton (11)	65
Sayuni Karunarathne (10)	66
Tommy Ruthven (10)	67
Nathan Doyle (11)	68
Thomas Finch (10)	69
Kuba Kotula (10)	70
Ella Brown (11)	71
Struan Fairbairn (10)	72
Tyler Ford (10)	73
Louis Brown (10)	74
Lewis O'Hare (10)	75

Harrytown Catholic High School, Romiley

Audrey Ubboe (12)	76

Heathfield Primary School, Handsworth

Aisha Siddiqa (11)	77
Fataha Akter (11)	78

Hermitage Primary School, Holmes Chapel

Lucy Walker (10)	79
Roxanne Bailey (10)	80

Kimbolton Primary Academy, Kimbolton

Paige Rowland (9)	81
Harper Bradley (7)	82
Alice Donahue (8)	83

Leadgate Primary School, Consett

Ella Turner (9)	84
Kasey-may Lumsden (9)	85
Mila Connolly (9)	86

Little Bloxwich CE (VC) School, Little Bloxwich

Louisa MacDonald (10)	87
Elise Bond (10)	88

Little Hill Primary School, Little Hill

Archie Atkinson (9)	89
Darcy Young (9)	90

Loreburn Primary School, Dumfries

Iona Noble-Caughill (10)	92

Maesmarchog Primary School, Dyffryn Cellwen

Amelia Williams (10)	93

Middleton-On-The-Wolds CE VC Primary School, Driffield

Lola-Rose Gill (8)	94
Bridget Fisher (7)	95

Mill Lane Junior Infant & Early Years School, Batley

Fatima Zahra Khan (10)	96

Oriel Academy West London, Hanworth

Zukhruf Ashrafi (10)	97
Zainab Fatima (10)	98
Tuanna Ucar (9)	100
Safa Shirzad (9)	101
Laura Esposito Vieira (10)	102
Emilisa Qinami (9)	103
Amira Butt (9)	104
Kacey Farinha (9)	105
Liana Qinami (10)	106
David Karl Morales (10)	107

Park Lane Primary School, Whittlesey

Vanessa Kosciecha (10)	108
Olivia Fitzjohn (10)	109
Sophie Fitzjohn (10)	110

Penboyr Church In Wales Voluntary Aided Primary School, Llandysul

Florence Mountain (10)	111

Pickhill CE Primary School, Thirsk

Millie Stanyer (7)	112

Rawdhatul Uloom Primary School, Burnley

Inara Daud (10)	113
Izzadeen Hussain (9)	114
Shihab Al Din (9)	115
Rugaya Kabir (9)	116
Laseebah Raees (10)	117
Muhammed Khizar Khan (10)	118

Rosslyn Park Primary And Nursery School, Aspley

Esther Adegoke (9)	119
Mariama Lisse Kane (10)	120
Florence-Richard Okezie (10)	121
Wealth Lazzerini (10)	122
Grace Adefarasin (9)	123

Sir Frederick Gibberd College, Harlow

Amelia Brearey (12)	124

Spittal C.i.W. V.C. School, Spittal

Edie Snelle (7)	125
Maci Williams (9)	126
Elijah John (7)	128
Thomas Bennet (7)	129
Alfie Hawkins (8)	130

St Alphonsus RC Primary School, Old Trafford

Tsz Tung Elizabeth Cheung (9)	131
Savannah Walker-Moore (10)	132

St Andrew's CE (VA) Primary School, Fontmell Magna

Indie Brown (8)	133
Greta Briars (8)	134
Oscar Iles (8)	135

St Bernard's RC Primary School, Ellesmere Port

Andrea Okodugha (9)	136

St Catherine Of Siena RC Primary School, Lee Bank

Aurora Chan (11)	137
AJ Kabuta (9)	138
Michelle Rajan (9)	139
Andrew Poon (9)	140
Saahiti Nagumalli (9)	141
Eliana Asfaw (10)	142
Letizia Lee (10)	143
Angela Liu	144

St Catherine's Preparatory School, Bramley

Victoria Lowe (9)	145
Madeleine Carlborg (9)	146
Caitlin Irons (8)	147
Hana Harding (9)	148
Felicity McMorrow (8)	149
Ines Wong (8)	150
Alexis Chan (8)	151
Ariana Diaz (8)	152
Beatrix Woodroffe (9)	153
Olivia Irvine (8)	154
Katrina Tam (10)	155
India Dhew (9)	156
Isabella Jones (8)	157
Zahra Bisi (9)	158

St George's CE Primary School, Langton Matravers

Rafe Jubber (9)	159
Elowen Hoad (7)	160

St Gerard's RC Primary School, Castle Vale

Isabella Wood (9)	161

St Gilbert's RC Primary School, Winton

Robyn Bland (10)	162

St John The Baptist CE (C) Primary School, Waltham Chase

Lily Hammond (8)	163
Scarlett Blake (8)	164

St Peter's Catholic Primary School, Dagenham

Nicole Chizitere Eke (10)	165
Alex Chima Eke (7)	166

St Stephen Churchtown Academy, St. Austell

Sophie Ledbrooke (8)	167

Stoke Minster CE Primary Academy, Stoke-On-Trent

Abdul Hannan (10)	168

The Blessed Sacrament Catholic Primary School, Ribbleton

Charis Antiaye (10)	169

The Marton Academy, Marton

Charlene Charley (8)	170

The Merton Primary School, Leicester

Serenity Gracie-Mai Irwin (8)	171
Skyla Stretton (8)	172
Quinn Evelyn Goff (9)	173
Riya Patel (8)	174

The Ridgeway Primary School, Reading

Nevaeh Asongo-Cassell (10)	175
Ayra Mohamed Ashif (9)	176
Phoebe Nunn (9)	177
Evelyn Carroll (9)	178
Katelin Krasniqi (9)	179
Evie Hewett (9)	180
William Robinson (9)	181
Levi Potter (9)	182
Yomola Erinoso (9)	183
Izabela Banas (9)	184
Latoya Ndlovu (9)	185
Isla Snarey (9)	186
Jewel Awhana (9)	187
Eli Murphy (9)	188
Calista Kwan (9)	189
Samaira Sharma (9)	190

The White House Preparatory School, London

Hiyori Minakawa (8)	191

Willow Green Academy, Ferrybridge

Logan Taylor (8)	192

**Wycliffe CE Primary School,
Shipley**

Molly Bishop (10)

THE CREATIVE WRITING

My Best Friend

My best friend is as beautiful as a rose
With green, beautiful eyes as green as green grass
With gold freckles as gold as a crown
With pink lips as pink as flamingo feathers
With her love of purple, like purple grapes
And her admiration for seals, like white feathers
Who has green eyes, golden freckles, pink lips, a love of purple and a love of seals?
My best friend.

Nerea Morente (9)
Abbey Gate College, Saighton

Untitled

If I am a star, there is plenty on me.
I am close to the planets, but not too close, otherwise the planets will burn.
I make light, day and night, for the Earth.
If people look at me, their eyes will be light.
What am I?

Answer: I am the sun.

Aurélien Desindes (8)
Albyn School, Aberdeen

The Three Cats

There was a cat,
He had a hat,
Which was long and black,
Like the second cat's sack,
The third cat broke his back,
By being in a sack,
Plus his name was Jack,
When the cat went whack,
He broke his back.

Magnus Foy (10)
Albyn School, Aberdeen

Windy Woods

In the horrible, haunting, windy woods,
There is a stomping beast,
That searches and seeks, through rivers and creeks,
For a crunchy, midnight feast.

In the horrible, haunting, windy woods,
A phoenix soars again,
With crackling, orange, feathered flames,
Disintegrates and then...

The haunting of All Hallow's Eve,
Brings all the myths alive,
They roam the woods, collecting screams,
To see their stories thrive.

These are the beasts of books and tales,
Told to rattle your bones,
At first they live in dreams alone,
Until they creep into your homes.

Connie Gregson (10)
Amesbury CE Primary School, Amesbury

The Dragon And The Witch

Deep among the trees
On a carpet made of leaves
There's a dragon snoring loudly
And a witch is laughing proudly
She casts a wicked spell
At the ringing of a bell
The dragon jumps, surprised
And blinks his yellow eyes
The fight begins at night
And goes on till the light
The witch lights up the sky
And the dragon flies up high
The sun is slowly rising
As if it is advising
Saying, "Your work here is done
You both have had your fun
Now go back to your home
And leave each other alone"
So neither of them win
And a calmer time begins.

Ottilie Gregson (7)
Amesbury CE Primary School, Amesbury

Space

S pectacular like the sun
P lanets floating like mesmerising fish in a pond
A liens soaring in big ships like fast-moving Frisbees
C olossal gas planets swerve in the air like the blades on a turbine on a breezy summer day
E arth is a wonderful planet, just like the people on it.

Matthew Craddock (10)
Aspin Park Community Primary, Knaresborough

Beware Of The Bear

Beware this Friday night
You could be in for a fright
Who's hiding upstairs?
A creepy bear
Could this be Fred Bear?
No, he is under the stairs
Maybe it's a scare bear?
Turn the lights off if you dare!

Morgan Hamilton (10)
Aspin Park Community Primary, Knaresborough

Stealing Our Land

We animals all knew that impending sadness would soon riddle our lands.
When the humans came,
They cut down our trees.

We all believe their sole purpose in their annoyingly long life is devoted
To killing us.

Over the years, we hid in trees,
Now we scram, as our homes get chopped
Carved,
And sold for 50% off.

Word on the street is that they're stealing our land,
I didn't believe them until I experienced it firsthand,
Successively, we lose our homes, and our forests are scattered with our bones.

Maltreatment and chopping down our trees is all they do,
Killing us off,
Some without a clue.

All they care about is money, and investments to make more money.

However, these 'smart' things haven't figured out that by doing this they're hurting
Themselves,
So it's in their interest to stop.

They're malicious creatures creating havoc for us and themselves,
Their elaborate plan is an evil scam,
We sometimes contemplate fighting back,
But we've never come around to doing so.

Sophia Diamond (10)
Belhaven Hill School, Dunbar

Behind The Door

Down to the third floor
Through the wooden door
Behind the old panel of wood
Would you enter if you could?
Behind the door.

Behind the door
A mossy floor
Branches blowing in the breeze
Mountains stretching above the trees
Behind the door.

Little kids skipping in the hills
Any sadness in you this world kills
A bubbling stream
This world is your dream
Behind the door.

In this world, it's summer all around
Daisies and tulips popping up from the ground
This is the distant far away land
All in the palm of your hand
This is all behind the door!

Alice Lindsay (11)
Belhaven Hill School, Dunbar

The Isle Of Tiree

Crisp, blue skies
The clearest sea
It's got it all on the Isle Of Tiree
Lie on the beach
Tan in the sun
Play on the beach and have some fun.

Surf on the waves
Sleep on the shore
Look for shells
Who can find more?

Ride on a boat
Race on the beach
Climb on the rocks
Watch the birds as they move in flocks.

So, now you know about the Isle Of Tiree
Come and have some fun and swim in the sea.

Holly Hutchison (10)
Belhaven Hill School, Dunbar

Monster Mystery

There's a monster hiding behind a bush,
Where a bug is just about to be smushed.
Hungry and dreadful he went to hunt in the forest with his bat,
He came home with an ant!

Still hungry he went lurking in the woods.
Falling into a patch of mud,
You can hear a loud thud.
Yelling with pain it felt as if he went insane.

Maira Usman (10)
Bolton Parish Church CE Primary School, Bolton

The Elephant Who Broke Our School

It was a calm and serene morning
And, with an enormous scream
An elephant barged in, causing a scene
Then, with another loud call
The whole pack came barging into the hall.

One ran outside and, with one big flip
The shed fell into a pile of sticks.

The others ran to the staffroom door
Destroying the library on all floors
"No! No! Not my library!" shouted Miss Gursoy
"No! No! Not my books, not my chairs."
"Don't take that, you... you trunked thing!" added Miss Wylie.

"You're paying for all this damage, you know!"

So take a bow
Because I don't know where I'm going to drink my coffee now!

Naimah Hussain (10)
Bonneygrove Primary School, Cheshunt

The Monsters That Came To Town

The day the monsters came to town,
Everything started to crumble down,
They all acted like a clown,
And for some reason, they wore a crown.

The monsters began to smash.
They then began to bash.
They even started to crash into the buildings,
And it would have cost a lot of cash to repair the damage.

Residents started to scream,
The scene was extreme,
Some people thought it was a dream,
There wasn't a gleam of hope for the police.

They started to smack,
The buildings all began to crack,
The monsters were on track,
They weren't going to turn back.

The trio headed down every street,
The monsters faced no sign of defeat,

The zombie began to eat,
It tasted like a treat.

Dracula and the mummy joined in with a crunch,
The whole lot were starting to munch,
The whole lot were in a bunch,
And they were eating things like it was lunch.

The monsters were going to blast,
Buildings were tumbling down fast,
The amount of space cleared was vast,
The monsters were done at last.

All of the buildings were about to fall,
Many people started to ghoul,
Lots of residents were on a call,
Though they didn't mean any harm at all.

Although they had committed such a naughty crime,
It was only for their friend Frankenstein,
They had a great time,
But then the army started to arrive.

Joshua Kimani (9)
Bonneygrove Primary School, Cheshunt

The New Girl In My School

There was a new person in my school
I wanted to be friends because she was cool
She blends with the ocean or maybe a potion
But there isn't any motion.

So
She is breathtakingly great
She is so cool
The girl who came
The girl who came
The girl who came to our school

Some said she was a plum
Her birthday is in July and she has blue eyes
People glared and stared but she didn't care

Wow
She is breathtakingly great
She is so cool
The girl who came
The girl who came
The girl who came to our school

She was shy but did not mind
She ate rice but she was kind

Love and care that was so fair
But you need to love yourself
You are perfect after all
And so cool, love yourselves
Not just everyone else

Love yourself
Love yourself
So just love yourself.

Lexi Khan-Vigus (10)
Bonneygrove Primary School, Cheshunt

The Lizard Who Made A Blizzard

The lizard came to call,
He went right through the entrance hall,
On top of the roof and all,
Right past the dining hall,
Finally in the science ball,
The big ray snapped,
It made him huge.

So...
He's absolutely great,
He's undeniably cool,
The lizard who made,
The lizard who made,
The lizard who made a blizzard.

He smashed the shed,
The playground fence,
Crashed and bashed the boy who had a rash,
And quickly dashed.

The headteacher panicked,
The chef got eaten
He thought they were to eat,

A nice, tasty treat,
He swung the tail round and round,
And then the first ever,
Lizard to make a blizzard.

Adam Chaudhry (9)
Bonneygrove Primary School, Cheshunt

The Bears Who Demolished The Park

The day the bears went to the park, they crashed,
The slide, the swing and the walls and dashed,
The families cried, "Help us!" then they got smashed,
And pieces of material were flying away as they got bashed,
Too far away.

"He's undeniably great,
He's utterly cool,"
The bears who demolished,
The bears who demolished,
The bears who demolished the park.

It didn't matter what they screamed,
It sounded like they were in a dream,
In utter shock,
They made a flock,
They were in a panic,
They thought it was manic,
The bears destroyed it all,
All there was, was soil on it all.

Noah Michael (10)
Bonneygrove Primary School, Cheshunt

The Day The Giraffe Came To Creams

The day the giraffe came to Creams
All the people thought they were having dreams
"What's he doing here?" all the people screamed
He bashed and smashed
Through the wall, he thought it was a ball
He was having a blast
Till it was time
He spun around and touched the ground
He left with a sneeze and in came bees
But...
He was undeniably great
He was absolutely cool
The giraffe who crashed
The giraffe who bashed
The giraffe who crashed Creams
He went to the seats
And went on his knees
And ate some cheese
And that was the story of the giraffe.

Grace McMullins (10)
Bonneygrove Primary School, Cheshunt

Rhino Rampage

R ampage breaks out through the school
H ere it comes into the hall
I nside lies a rhino's call
N ow here it comes, by the playground wall
O n the other side lies a ball, music playing until a squall.

R ampage breaks out through the hall
A mongst the crowd, people squall
M oment by moment, people cry
P eople shout, "God, why?"
A nd moment by moment, the ball goes dry
"G od" people cry
E xit was the only option, so that's what people try.

Jake Timson (9)
Bonneygrove Primary School, Cheshunt

The Day The Rhino Demolished Tesco!

The rhino started smashing down the doors
Crashing into glass and dashing through aisles
He started eating people, crushing people and didn't stop.

So...
He's undeniably mean
He's absolutely vicious
The rhino who ate
The rhino who ate
The rhino who ate Tesco.

He sat on people shopping
He made children cry
And broke the bathroom doors.

So...
He's undeniably mean
He's absolutely vicious
The rhino who ate
The rhino who ate
The rhino who ate Tesco.

Sydney Spink (9)
Bonneygrove Primary School, Cheshunt

The Rhino Who Broke Into Our School

The day the rhino came to school,
He drank the water from the public pool,
And broke into the enormous wall,
And slate by slate the roof and all,
The staffroom, gym and entrance hall.

So, he's undeniably great,
He's absolutely cool,
The rhino who broke,
The rhino who broke,
The rhino who broke into our school.

People panicked, teachers ran,
They didn't know what to do with a rhino on their land.
He suddenly chewed through the lollipop man,
Three parked cars and a transit van.

Elif Michalski (9)
Bonneygrove Primary School, Cheshunt

The Snake Who Devoured The School

The day the snake came to school
They swallowed the gate and swallowed the hall
And all the rooms and shows
So she's undeniably great
She's absolutely cool

The snake who devoured
The snake who devoured
The snake who devoured the school

She swallowed Miss D's books, even her hooks and she slithered with a quiver
And left a wreck, "Oh no, not my shed," said Miss Sharp
It was in rubble and pipes and shovels until a dragon came to school
Oh no, not again.

Lily-Mae Catlin (9)
Bonneygrove Primary School, Cheshunt

The Clumsy Rhino

It was Monday morning, calm and curbed,
Then something enormous disturbed,
They walk the ball like a swimming pool,
And called with a bit of rule.

He tumbled into Barry, but also Garry,
A family shouted, "A rhino charged into the shop,"
What a shock.

Tommy crashed,
Connor dashed,
The cleaners smashed,
Baba crashed.

They thought it was done,
The rhino blinked in the midday sun,
He gave one last sneeze,
They were all on their knees.

Olivia Walsh (8)
Bonneygrove Primary School, Cheshunt

The Panda Rampage

The day the panda came to call, it went to the food hall
It went past the employees then past the trollies
He fell and hit a bell
He stepped on some stocks then tripped on some socks

He bashed and crashed and smashed in some trash
He was walking around and heard a crunch
And it was a bunch of munch

Well...
He's undeniably great
He's absolutely cool
The panda who wrecked
The panda who wrecked
The panda who wrecked M&S.

Alex Harling (9)
Bonneygrove Primary School, Cheshunt

Untitled

C hildren are brats, they scurry like rats,
H aving fun, they never run, not even in the sun.
I nkland will be free and then we'll have some tea.
L aughter makes me sick; it makes me want to throw a stick.
D ogs' droppings! They smell like poo, just like in the loo!
R unning and falling, screaming and crying,
E verything will be all right; they'll never be in sight.
N ever to be seen again.

Sophie Schuster (9)
Bonneygrove Primary School, Cheshunt

The Elephant That Crushed M&S

The day the elephant came to call, she crushed the clothes and the entrance hall and all the food.
Only Brussels sprouts to be seen.
So,
She's undeniably great
She's absolutely cool
The elephant who crushed
The elephant who crushed
The elephant who crushed M&S.
She galloped her way out of the entrance hall.
She crushed the cars and the greens.
People ran with only fear in their bones.

Millie Brown (9)
Bonneygrove Primary School, Cheshunt

The Day The Tiger Came To School

I was at school,
In time-out,
Until I heard a vicious roar,
We looked out of the window,
Seeing a claw scratch the door,
The tiger scratched the walls with it,
The tiger who drank,
The tiger who drank,
The tiger who drank from our pool.

Wow...
He was undeniably great,
He was amazingly cool,
The tiger who drank,
The tiger who drank,
The tiger who drank from our pool!

Mira Ustun (9)
Bonneygrove Primary School, Cheshunt

Witches

W retched little brats, their laugh is like an endless screech in your mind... or is it in reality?
I n every crevice and crack, there is a revolting small child.
T reacherous tiny beasts, coming around your used-to-be-peaceful neighbourhood.
C reatures so very hideous they make me sick.
H orrid, filthy vermin, smelling like dogs' droppings always.

Orlagh Peet (9)
Bonneygrove Primary School, Cheshunt

Untitled

The day the dragon came to school
They drank the water from the pool
So
They're undeniably great
They're undeniably cool

The dragon who ate
The dragon who ate
The dragon who ate our school

But everybody panicked; the teachers screamed
Then one teacher disappeared
Then all of them vanished, and they were never seen again.

Dino Pacitti (9)
Bonneygrove Primary School, Cheshunt

The Snake That Struck School

The day the snake came to call,
Silver slime took over,
Pupils panicked, teachers ran,
She flew at them with a wide chomp,
She ate the staffroom, gym, and hall,
She said he was sad he was dead.

So...
She's undeniably great,
She's absolutely cool,
The snake who ate,
The snake who ate,
The snake who ate our school.

Hope Mcglynn (9)
Bonneygrove Primary School, Cheshunt

Witches

W retched children are little brats
I n every corner of my eye, I see one roaming the streets
T alking about them makes me feel sick
C reatures so vile should be wiped out from the Earth
H ideous pests are a plague and spread like a disease
E specially when they are at school
S o we need to get rid of them.

Libby Doughty (9)
Bonneygrove Primary School, Cheshunt

Children – A Witch's Viewpoint

C hildren are pesky little rats,
H ell is where they belong,
I n every corner, you see them having fun,
L et's turn this work into child-free,
D ead, they must be dead,
R evolting little pests,
E verywhere you go, you can smell their pesky stench,
N o one ever liked these rats.

Kacper Zuk (9)
Bonneygrove Primary School, Cheshunt

The Witch Who Came To School

The witch who came to school
She dashed
And crashed through the hall
She thought the children smelt of dog droppings
Like the teacher was mopping
Down the hall
The children are no fun
They make me want to turn and run.

Charlie Bickenstaff (9)
Bonneygrove Primary School, Cheshunt

Sad Nature

A cluster of ravens all gather together
To make the moment beautiful as a feather.
Separated from all, here lies a desperate man
Who is wanted now by all humans.

He just wanted to revive the wildlife
But he never did, all his life.
The habitats are vanishing, the trees are dying
Animals are leaving, birds aren't seen flying.

When will this ever stop?
He asked himself to reach the top.
It will last forever
Responded the mind, truthful as ever.

What humanity doesn't understand
Is that the Earth won't forever stand.
Solar flares will hit the surface
With which the plants will come face to face.

The magnetic field can't take it anymore
And the plant life will stay no more.
Victory for the evil, death for us
The solar flare will be humungous.

We should let him help and live
And then the environment will always live.
So will we. Revive the seas
Anything, like the Urmia Sea.

The habitats will stay, the trees will live
Animals will stay, birds will also live!
Now the government will know
Then everybody will know!

Soon, soon 'til it's 2040
Reaching net zero, good for the countries.
Great! Great! The ozone is great
Great! Our magnetic field is great!

Roshan Govind (9)
Brindishe Green Primary School, Hither Green

Rod

On a planet far from Earth called Crod
There was an alien by the name of Rod
Rod's species name was known as Zed
And he slept in something like a bed

He eats black grapes and drinks blue tea
And has three siblings, Jo, Jen and Fee
He lives with his mother, father and pet dog, Stena
Has two eyes, two legs but no antenna

One day Rod played a game of cricket
Then suddenly the ball turned into a biscuit
He flew away so he could see
Just where o where the biscuit could be

Next thing, he went to planet Mars
And saw some creatures they called Gars
He asked one Gar, "Have you seen a biscuit?"
"Yes," he said, "I found it in my rocket."

The Gar showed Rod his shiny rocket
And Rod said, "Let's fly and see the comet"
He landed home on planet Crod
And his family said, "Welcome back, Rod!"

Deio Earnshaw (11)
Bryngwran Primary School, Bryngwran

Earth

We all live around the Earth.
There are things, big things
And things that are small.
I can't name them all.
We all live on the Earth,
Above dirt. Everybody walks
On the Earth. Everybody talks
On the Earth in some way.
Everyone plays some days,
Until bedtime.
There are so many people
In the world, I can't count
Such a big amount.

The Earth is for everyone,
Nobody owns it, and they never will.
Earth is a place to be kind.

Mansaha Seidu (8)
Carswell Community Primary School, Abingdon

Growing Up

G rowing up can be hard,
R owing across life's hard times,
O wning things that might be special,
W hizzing through life's good times,
I n life there are changes; maybe good changes or bad changes
N ights you lie in bed dreaming,
G row and don't let anyone stop you.

U nhappy or happy still chase your dreams in life,
P op! We're all growing up.

Maisie Tutty (8)
Carswell Community Primary School, Abingdon

Rome

The Colosseum is a dome in Rome
And that is the thing for which I'm writing this poem.

Where gladiators fought lions and others, they showed 'em.
Where peasants got slain and the sun was always glowin'.

It doesn't matter who wins or loses,
The crowd was always full with cheers and boos.

The emperor was sat in the royal booth
Whereas the poor were sat high up in the bird poos.

In the arena it was a free-for-all,
There was literally not a single rule,
Fighting was even taught in school!
The Romans must've been really cruel.

But now the Romans are very old, all their bodies are stone-cold.
The Roman era lives on, truth be told
In things that we're selling across the world.

Aidan Skelton (11)
Copthorne Preparatory School, Copthorne

Seasons

Colours now seeping through,
As the sky turns a lovely hue,
Birds chirping all around,
The sound of bleating abounds.

The sun shines bright in the midday sky,
Beaches are packed as spirits run high,
Let's load up the car; school holidays are here,
Away we go travelling, as the children cheer.

Red, orange and yellow are revealing on the trees,
Can you feel the chill of the autumn breeze?
Birds flying high through the midnight sky,
Halloween is almost nigh.

All the leaves are now long gone,
And the bare branches are forlorn,
As Christmas approaches and the ground turns white,
Everyone waits for the magical night.

Sophia Berkovic (11)
Copthorne Preparatory School, Copthorne

The Mystery Queen

Let me tell you about my favourite queen,
One of the most famous England has ever seen.
Out of six, she was the second wife,
Who lived a short and tragic life.

She married one of the very worst kings,
A man who did unforgivable things.
He wanted a son, she had a daughter,
This is one of the reasons she was sent to the slaughter.

So angry he was, that he cut off her head,
But she was brave until her final words were said.
Her life was a terrible shame,
But with all these clues, do you know her name?

Anastasia Glover (9)
Copthorne Preparatory School, Copthorne

Poppy My Puppy

P oppy's floppy, cute, curly ears bounce when she runs and she looks adorable
O ut of all the puppies in the world, I think she is the sweetest and prettiest
P oppy's biting is quite hard, although I do like her hazel-brown eyes and wide-eyed tiny face
P oppy is so cute when her ears are back that I just want to give her a big squeeze
Y es, I love her very much.

Aurelia Pullen (9)
Countess Gytha Primary School, Queen Camel

Best Friends That Make Ends

I had a best friend.
I loved her to the very end.
She was kind and had a gentle mind until,
We grew older and her spirit grew bolder.
She was sharp as a blade.
We grew distant, wanted action and said I was a distraction.
She threw me away when all I wanted to ever do was play.
Made me feel the empty grey of a rainy day.
When she realised we were apart,
It shot her in the heart.
So we are back together
To have a friendship that will last forever.

Grace Long (10)
Dalton School, Dalton

Six Years

Year one was fun
Year two was cool,
Take a look at all the things we drew
Three and four was a war
Going to lunch was a hunch
Four had MTC on top of Bronte's trip
Five and six gonna be quick
High school coming like a boulder
Six had SATs
Don't try hacks
All this time making friends
I think I see the end
Wow, the past was a blast.

Jessica Stevenson (10)
Dean Field Community Primary School, Ovenden

Peeno, Peeno, Peeno

Peeno, Peeno, Peeno,
Go wear your clean clothes,
You haven't showered in a year,
And been screaming in my ears,
There's mud on your face,
You little disgrace,
Now go sell the cows,
No, not your little brother,
Go to your aunt,
And say this cake is from your mother.

Peeno, Peeno, Peeno,
Can't you just listen this once?
We're going to the shops,
So go put your coat on,
Peeno, Peeno, Peeno,
You spent £5,000 worth of peanuts,
But you're a peanut!
Mom stands for 'Made Of Money' you say?
When your father gets home,
You will have nothing to say.

So that was the end of Peeno, I guess,
Now his mum is happy and free of stress.

Maheen Shamoon (11)
Dixons Allerton Academy, Allerton

Outer Space

There are nine planets
That orbit the sun,
But people and animals
Live on just one.

The Earth is our planet,
We must take good care of the air
Land and water, that all people
Must share.

The sun keeps us warm
Wherever we are,
All our light comes
From this great big star.

A rocket's the best way
To travel in space,
With one great big blast
You can go any place!

Astronauts travel
A long way through space,
They learn lots of facts
That they bring back to base.

One, two, three, four, five, six, seven, eight, nine, ten,
blast off!

Hiba Javed (10)
Dixons Allerton Academy, Allerton

Untitled

In the wild, where creatures roam free
From the buzzing bee to the grand tall tree
Each animal dances in nature's grand play
A symphony of life in bright hues of grey
The lion's proud roar echoes through the night
While the gentle deer grazes in the morning light
The dolphin leaps higher, a joyous ballet
As the wise old owl watches night turning to day
With fur, fins and feathers, each one has a role
In the circle of life, they all make us whole
So let's celebrate animals, both big and small
For in their wild beauty, we find joy in it all.

Sophie MCDonnell (9)
Downpatrick Primary School, Downpatrick

Friends

Friends are people you can trust,
They can help you,
Love you and care for you.
They are kind and friendly,
And can share stuff with you,
They are always there for you,
To help you when you need it.
Friends are amazing,
And it's good to have some.

Katherine Napier (10)
Downpatrick Primary School, Downpatrick

Winter

Winter is coming, snow is falling,
The night is dark, the wind is calling.
The hedgehogs are hibernating underground,
Not many creatures can be found.
It's a cold, dark night,
The moon shines bright.
The trees are bare,
No leaves live there.
Owls fly through the sky,
The cold wind flies by.
Out come the hats, scarves and gloves,
There are games that everyone loves.
Everyone comes out to play,
In the snow every day.
Collecting mistletoe and holly,
Winter's a time it's really jolly.
Santa's coming on his reindeer,
With toys for everyone, don't fear.
Winter is coming, snow is falling,
The night is dark, the wind is calling.

Tara Hawker (7)
English Bicknor CE (VC) Primary School, English Bicknor

The Universe Of Wonder

An array of twinkling stars shine bright,
Within the crystal-clear, cloudless night.

The crescent moon fills the sky,
As flocks of birds soar silently by.

Spiraling galaxies can be seen,
In elegant swirls of red and green.

Gargantuan planets orbit like the Earth,
Billions of years since their birth.

As dawn arrives and starts to glisten,
The universe wakes and stops to listen.

Max Slater (11)
Featherstone All Saints CofE Academy, North Featherstone

Man's Best Friend

He gets excited when I walk through the door
He sits down and hands me his paw

He loves to chase a ball
He always returns at my call

He loves to bark at the cats
He likes to sit on people's laps

He loves cuddles at night
He sits with me under the light

He always helps me calm my fear
He is always there when I shed a tear

He was there when I met my wife
He has been with me his whole life

He comes with me everywhere I go
He especially likes it in the snow

He likes to go on winter walks
He listens to my worries but never talks

I will be with him until the end
My dog, my love, man's best friend.

Aurora McMahon (10)
Flax Hill Junior Academy, Gillway

Secret Scales

Those secret scales,
Leave no trails,
Slither past, not a sound,
Nothing.

Until... In the dark,
Orange eyes glint,
Giving you a hint,
With a flicking tongue,
A snake lurks.

Zoey Broadfield (9)
Gawthorpe Community Academy, Gawthorpe

Roly Poly - Holy Moly!

Ancient creature, cute to some
Minibeasts look like they're having fun
Come over here, bro
To my humble home, dark and damp is the way to go.

My diet is weird so some will say
Eating food that's decayed
Mushy, rotten, slimy, wet
Munch munch munch. Yum? You bet!

14 legs watch me go scurrying, scuttling high and low
I have many names
Slaters, tiggy-hogs, pillbugs, chuggy pigs and more
Not bad for a humble creature who lives under the floor.

Meredith Reffin (8)
Greatwood Community Primary And Nursery School, Skipton

Running With The Wolves

The brilliant moon shining on the churning, running river
But the gigantic pines with spiky branches are silver
Slippery fish jump out of shallow water, the leaves shattering
The wolves' paws thudding on the dirty puddles, leaves scattering
Wagging tails dash past me howling and wailing
Fluffy, luffy, and scruffy wolves with exciting shrieking
The wolves' paws with shining claws and howling.

Liza Kruchinina (10)
Halyrude Primary School, Peebles

Spring's Arrival

You can hear a choir of birds,
Perched up on an oak tree,
But the air is still cold,
And your window is too foggy to see.

Icy snow melts away,
Young children come out to play,
"It's finally spring!" they all say.

The soil is moist,
With bright flowers beginning to rise up,
As you relax on your sofa,
Drinking morning tea from a cup.

Icy snow melts away,
Young children come out to play,
"It's finally spring!" they all say.

There are branches, leaves and fruit,
That now start to gradually grow,
As you take a walk,
And freeze your big toe.

Icy snow melts away,
Young children come out to play,
"It's finally spring!" they all say.

There are delightful delicate daisies,
And beautiful buzzing bees,
Spring is always full of life,
As far as anyone sees.

Icy snow melts away,
Young children come out to play,
"It's finally spring!" they all say.

But sadly, it's time for spring to end,
As it is summer's time to shine.
I hope you enjoyed your spring,
Because I certainly enjoyed mine.

Maria O'Hara (11)
Halyrude Primary School, Peebles

A Magical Year

In winter the snow falls from the roofs,
The smell of gingerbread fills the air,
The wonderful winter fair,
Winter is leaving.

The flowers start to bloom
Spring is finally here,
After a year,
The newly-born lambs,
And pink cherry blossom,
Perfectly-placed picnics,
On fluffy green grass,
Sadly spring has come to an end.

But summer is coming,
Children playing in the playful park,
You can hear the dogs bark,
Boat trips planned,
And holidays booked,
Watching the opalescent ocean,
While the summer sets,
August comes to an end.

September is here,
Harvesting pumpkins,

Decorated houses,
Halloween is here,
Spooky costumes everywhere.

Back to winter then New Year's Eve,
That's a year gone by,
Hope you have fun next year.

Sadie Noble (11)
Halyrude Primary School, Peebles

Forest Creek

Birds sing a sweet tune,
At night you can see the moon.
Animals drink from the creek,
Birds feed their babies from the beak.
In autumn, leaves fall
And become crunchy after all.
A pack of wolves prowl the night,
When animals see them, they get a fright.
Eagles soar over the towering trees,
Deep in the forest, there is a hive full of bees.

Ellie McCubbing (11)
Halyrude Primary School, Peebles

Halloween

I was sleeping like a dead old witch
When my golden light randomly switched
I woke up in a bloody haunted house
But I was hungry so I ate a mouse
I was walking in a dark hallway with a bad mood
But then an old, evil-looking dude said, "You taste good,"
A random, huge black creature chased me
While a goat was sitting and drinking tea.

Gosia Czuprynko (10)
Halyrude Primary School, Peebles

Growing Up

There's nothing to worry about when you're a kid
But when you're an adult you worry about taxes and how to bid
Live, laugh, love in your town
'Til the majestic moon comes up and the sun goes down
When you're a kid you're outside most of the time
When you're an adult you are at work all the time to earn a dime.

Jula Sidorjakova (10)
Halyrude Primary School, Peebles

October

October mornings are my favourite days
It always brings me joy to hear the birds chirping like they are singing
Hearing the autumn leaves as I step on them
Best of all are the foggy days covering my view like something on my glasses
The cold breeze in the air of the autumn skies
The autumn leaves falling from the trees.

Casey Morton (11)
Halyrude Primary School, Peebles

Fall Is Coming

Farmers harvesting pumpkins everywhere
To carve and decorate
Pumpkin pasties, pumpkin pies, and pumpkin spice
As the smell of tasty treats fills the air
Golden, amber, and scarlet leaves
Crunching everywhere
While the childish children begin to trick or treat
In the depths of the Halloween night.

Sayuni Karunarathne (10)
Halyrude Primary School, Peebles

The Gorgeous Guinea Pig

The gorgeous guinea pig is a chubby one
He loves fresh, juicy watermelons
His little pattering paws roam the grassy fields
As his friends pounce in joy
While the guinea pig plays with his toys
And then he sees his friend Squeak!
I think he deserves a treat.

Tommy Ruthven (10)
Halyrude Primary School, Peebles

Outer Space

I land on Mars,
I see a lot of stars,
I'm floating through space,
I'd rather do a rocket race,
There are a lot of colours in the Milky Way,
The moon is so grey,
I'm flying through space in my rocket,
I wish the astronaut suit had a pocket.

Nathan Doyle (11)
Halyrude Primary School, Peebles

Earth

The world can be sad,
But it can also be rad.

Now, Voyager One,
And Voyager Two.

Solar panels are fab,
But war is super sad.

There's no Planet B,
But there's only one planet Earth.

Thomas Finch (10)
Halyrude Primary School, Peebles

The Fluff One

Black and white fluff ball
Straight white whiskers on his nose
Poke me on the cheeks
He softly walks on the leaves
Hunting birds in the moonlight.

Kuba Kotula (10)
Halyrude Primary School, Peebles

The Start Of Spring

Things start to grow back
All the seeds are in brown sacks
Crops start to sprout now
See the squirrel run about
They screech and shout all around.

Ella Brown (11)
Halyrude Primary School, Peebles

The Skeleton

Rigid bones around
Bones falling off at night-time.
Scary but hard bones
Mouthful of teeth at night-time
Bony arms follow me.

Struan Fairbairn (10)
Halyrude Primary School, Peebles

Chemistry

Chemistry is great!
Beakers with liquid in them,
Liquid explosions,
Keep your safety glasses on!
Loud explosions everywhere.

Tyler Ford (10)
Halyrude Primary School, Peebles

Long Car Journey

Long car journey
You could try to find a person that likes long car trips
With the hot stuffy air and the expensive petrol.

Louis Brown (10)
Halyrude Primary School, Peebles

The Hamster

A haiku

Hamster Fluffabel
Is small, fluffy and cuddly
His rolls are crazy.

Lewis O'Hare (10)
Halyrude Primary School, Peebles

Frog Prince

In a land so far away.
A princess bright as day,
Met a frog in dismay,
A prince in strange array.

With a heart so kind and true,
She knew just what to do,
Kissed the frog, no ado,
A prince emerged; anew.

Together they found delight,
In love's pure and bright light,
The princess and prince, just right,
A tale of magic, shining bright.

Audrey Ubboe (12)
Harrytown Catholic High School, Romiley

Yummy Tomatoes

Oh ho what a wonderful tomato,
Oh ho what a wonderful sight,
One day a mouse ate it and ran away like a flash,
Oh ho what a wonderful tomato,
Oh ho what a wonderful wind,
One day a man ate it and ran away for free, he even shakes the bear as happy as candy,
Oh ho what a wonderful tomato,
Oh ho what a wonderful tomato,
Oh ho what a wonderful wind.

Aisha Siddiqa (11)
Heathfield Primary School, Handsworth

You Are My Best Friend

You are my best friend,
Our friendship never ends,
We do everything together,
And that's forever,
We share every tear
And face each other's fear,
You know how I feel,
'Cos we're on the same wheel,
You are my best friend
And my only best friend.

Fataha Akter (11)
Heathfield Primary School, Handsworth

Winter

I could feel the cold surrounding my toes,
Holding them in its icy embrace,
My scarf wrapped tightly around my nose,
The blue in the sky slowly faded to grey.

The once-melted snow was back again,
Seeking its frosty revenge,
The leaves on the trees could no longer be seen,
I watched the shivering robins starting to preen.

The wind whispered in the silence,
The flowers waited to bloom again with patience,
The once wild river was now still,
The icicles dangling from the trees glistened like diamonds.

A thick blanket of snow covered the forest,
The animals went and slept in every corner and crevice,
Each hollow tree became a bed for a weary badger,
Every unturned log became a home for a desperate woodlouse,
The forest seemed lifeless, except for me.

Lucy Walker (10)
Hermitage Primary School, Holmes Chapel

My Unique Colour Cat

My unique cat is very colourful
She roams around the streets
Others stop and stare
To see all the colours
Purple, blue, yellow, orange
The unique cat loves to dance
On the streets
Others join her as she puts a smile on everyone's face
Then one day someone asks, "Why all the colour and dancing?"
To be told we're all different in a way
Black, white, blue, yellow
We all dance on our paws together
To put a smile on your face
Brings joy and happiness to a good, unique cat.

Roxanne Bailey (10)
Hermitage Primary School, Holmes Chapel

Out There

Cosmic dust, dark matter and black holes are all out there
What is out there?
Planet rings made of ice, sand and space debris
Can I make a cake in space? No, but you can see the dwarf planet
Can I swim in space? Yes, the whole galaxy is made of very thin water
What's your favourite colour? Blue!
Well you'll see plenty of blue out there on sunsets on Mars
What is out there?

Paige Rowland (9)
Kimbolton Primary Academy, Kimbolton

Happy

H appy is what all of us want to be so turn your frowns upside down
A ll emotions are good but happy is the one that you should have
P eople dancing, people laughing, that's what I want to see
P enguins should be happy when they get their food. They are happy and you should be happy too
Y ou're happy, I am happy, everybody is happy.

Harper Bradley (7)
Kimbolton Primary Academy, Kimbolton

Pablo

P ablo's favourite food is peanut butter
A playful puppy
B ecause he is so cute
L oving him starts when you see him
O bservant, likes to find little things.

Alice Donahue (8)
Kimbolton Primary Academy, Kimbolton

Teachers Are Always Great

A great teacher is irreplaceable.
They should have a special place in every child's heart.
You are so kind. You give me peace and joy.
You're my teacher and you're the best.
When God made teachers he gave us special friends,
When I started school that day seemed so far away.
The beauty and the wonder of everything.
We see a special gift for learning and a heart that deeply cares.
You owe a lot of love to them.
I shall applaud.
I express to them my gratitude for instilling in me a wonderful attitude.
Let this message remind you that you are special through and through.
Thank you for being there.
You're the best of every class teacher.
The soul of every school.
Your work is a work of art.
Thank you, teacher, for being my life's role model.
You taught us the best.
Now is the time to say thank you.
You are the best.

Ella Turner (9)
Leadgate Primary School, Consett

As The Leaves Fall

When the wind whistles and the leaves fall,
What is that word we call?
When the fire gets turned on,
And the porridge is in the pan,
What is that word? I just don't understand?
When the wellies are on,
And we hear the sound of leaves,
I wonder what this could mean?
Warm scarves,
Woolly hats,
Hot cocoa,
And warm friendly chats,
As the leaves fall I hear the wind call,
The special word I've been looking for,
Autumn
Autumn is here!
Let us all give a big cheer.

Kasey-may Lumsden (9)
Leadgate Primary School, Consett

IDK

IDK why we broke up
IDK how to make up
IDK how I got like this
IDK why he had to cheat
IDK why I let him slide for all this time
So I'm heartbroken!
The pain, he gave me pain mentally and physically
IDK why I got with him.

Mila Connolly (9)
Leadgate Primary School, Consett

The Animal Farm

Down on the farm on a lovely sunny day,
Go to the animal farm and with the animals play,
See cat, hamster, dog, cow, horse and sheep,
Then watch the animals go to sleep.

It's a very unusual sight to see,
As all the animals climb up the tree,
On the day of the race,
The squirrel they chase.

And what is very silly about this space,
Is the animals run the place,
When they have babies of their own,
They will share this lovely home.

Down on the farm on a lovely sunny day,
Go to the animal farm and with the animals play,
See cat, hamster, dog, cow, horse and sheep,
Then watch the animals go to sleep.

Louisa MacDonald (10)
Little Bloxwich CE (VC) School, Little Bloxwich

Bluebells

Bluebells oh bluebells
Oh heavenly bluebells
The peaceful aroma
With its lovely smells

Go cantering through
On my lovely pony
The beautiful sight
I never feel lonely

Just me and my pony
Nice bluebells line the track
The birds slowly chime
I do not want to pack

Finally, we go home
What a beautiful day
Oh no, look at the time
I got carried away.

Elise Bond (10)
Little Bloxwich CE (VC) School, Little Bloxwich

Space Voyage

One day, far away, a rocket went to space,
Gravity it did defy, whizzing from place to place.
It flew through the solar system and glided past the planets,
It zoomed through the Milky Way and narrowly avoided comets.

The rocket touched down on the moon,
Not too late and not too soon.
The spaceman leapt out and planted his flag
And collected some moon rocks in his bag.

The journey home was smooth and fast,
Who knew the universe was so vast?
All the sights he must have seen,
Oh, what fun it must have been!

Archie Atkinson (9)
Little Hill Primary School, Little Hill

The Baby Whale

One day in the dark blue sea
A whale was born as small as can be
Even though the whale was small
She knew she would grow tall
On the whale's birthday party
The party was arty
When the whale was older
She tried to find a lover
And she wanted to become a mother
But she could not become a mother
Because she could not find a lover
One day she got a letter
She was invited to the ocean ball; this couldn't be better
She went to go and buy a dress
To become the prettiest princess
The carriage she called was too small
She called another carriage
But all she wanted was marriage
When she said her goodbye
The prince arrived
The prince then chose her as the winner
But she felt she had to be thinner

The prince liked her for who she was
Then they fell in love
Then they had children
And their children had grandchildren
This was the best day of their lives
They all lived happily ever after.

Darcy Young (9)
Little Hill Primary School, Little Hill

Friends Will Argue

Friends will argue, no matter what,
Every now and then but not too much.
I know it hurts, I've had them too,
But if you wait patiently, they will come back to you.
Life is tough, but you'll get through it,
But with good friends, you can push through it.

Iona Noble-Caughill (10)
Loreburn Primary School, Dumfries

Dream In Space

Space is a dream,
One that you've never seen.
You use a spoon to eat the cheese moon
It tastes so good
So share it with the neighbourhood
The black hole can suck up your soul
We're so small compared to the Earth's ball
The Milky Way, I can talk about it all day
It's where the Earth is, and that's where we live
It's so relaxing floating in space
You can touch stars
It's not fair to see you floating
I'm the air
It's so fun to jump and run on the moon with a spoon.

Amelia Williams (10)
Maesmarchog Primary School, Dyffryn Cellwen

Two Girls Called Daisy And Charlotte

Friendship is caring and sharing, loving and supporting
Understanding and being understood
Bear hugs and belly laughs
Comfortable in total silence
The poetry of life
The icing on the cake
The glue that holds the world together
Crazy adventures and happy memories
Laughing, laughing and more laughing
Chatting about nothing much for hours on end
A listening ear and a shoulder to cry on
A very special blessing from God
Having someone you can call at 3am
Friendship makes the good times better and the hard times a little easier
Friendship is not a big thing, it is a billion little things
Thank you so much for being a totally amazing friend.

Lola-Rose Gill (8)
Middleton-On-The-Wolds CE VC Primary School, Driffield

Moon

The moon's right there in the bright, night sky,
I start to cry, but I don't know why,
Maybe it's because I love the moon,
And I hope it visits me soon,
The moon's right there in the bright, night sky.

Bridget Fisher (7)
Middleton-On-The-Wolds CE VC Primary School, Driffield

The Harvest Moon

The harvest moon resting in bed,
Drifting to his slumber sleep,
While emptying his head,
Shining like a rare gem.

As the leaves fall,
The moon shines like a glowing ball,
Black day, black night,
Halloween's back, don't get a fright.

Squirrels scurry and birds fly,
Ghosts are back, but please don't cry,
Animals have hibernated,
As the moonlight moon shows them where to go.

The harvest moon resting in bed,
Drifting to his slumber sleep,
While emptying his head,
Shining like a rare gem.

Fatima Zahra Khan (10)
Mill Lane Junior Infant & Early Years School, Batley

Out Of This World

In the night sky, the moon is a big cheese
Dancing around stars with the greatest of ease
Wearing pyjamas all fluffy and bright
He chuckles at Earth through the blanket of night

I've seen all your bunnies and your buddy old frogs
Even those dancing with sparkly dogs
But up here in space, it's all just a breeze
While you race your cars and you itch for peas

So next time you gaze at the big lunar scoop
Remember the moon is a giggly loop
Just having fun while we sleep snugly in our bed
Dreaming of cheese wheels and space food ahead!

Zukhruf Ashrafi (10)
Oriel Academy West London, Hanworth

Deep In The Rainforest

Deep in the rainforest, deep in the rainforest, what did I see?
What did I see? I saw a monkey,
Swinging tree to tree.
Deep in the rainforest, deep in the rainforest, what did I see?
What did I see? I saw a parrot,
Flying vine to vine.

Deep in the rainforest, deep in the rainforest, what did I hear?
What did I hear? I heard squirrels
Making a sound.
Deep in the rainforest, deep in the rainforest, what did I hear?
What did I hear? I heard a bird,
Singing a song.

Deep in the rainforest, deep in the rainforest, what did I smell?
What did I smell? I smelt a rose,
Which had a beautiful smell.

Deep in the rainforest, deep in the rainforest, what did I smell?
What did I smell? I smelt some fresh fruits,
Hanging on the trees.

Zainab Fatima (10)
Oriel Academy West London, Hanworth

The Halloween Fright

The fright, a Halloween night,
Taunting spirits creep in the dim moonlight,
Wolves' howls echo swiftly through the skies,
As the full moon begins to rise.

Crowds of ecstatic children scatter from door to door,
They scream, "Trick or treat!"
Giggle and roar in their costumes so wicked and creepy,
Not a single soul is an ounce of sleepy.

As the clock strikes twelve *beware!*
Silhouettes lurking in the sombre shadows dare to scare,
Whispered tales must not reach the light,
On this frightful Halloween night.

Tuanna Ucar (9)
Oriel Academy West London, Hanworth

Alone In The Amazon Rainforest

It is night, pitch-black night
A sliver of moon invisible through the shutters
Shines against the wood
My room without light encloses me like a blanket
Thick, dark, and formless
Cocooned in my hammock I hear sounds
The crunch of leaves
The whoosh of wings
Croaks and hoots
Cries, shrieks and whistles
Wooden boards creak
Sutters shake
A low, heavy breathing keeps me awake
Until exhaustion, stroking my skin, relaxes my muscles
And pressing softly against my heavy eyelids
Sends me into the darkness
Alone.

Safa Shirzad (9)
Oriel Academy West London, Hanworth

Me And My Cool Friend

I have this cool friend
In my awesome school
Oh the time we spend
Yes, she's super cool

We know everything about each other
I know she likes yellow,
She knows I like marshmallow
And we both have one similarity
We both love butter

She hosts loads of sleepovers
Our life is like a roller coaster
She braids my hair
But I wouldn't dare
She thinks that's fair
I know our friendship will never end
Because of me and my cool friend.

Laura Esposito Vieira (10)
Oriel Academy West London, Hanworth

My Paradise

A homeland of delusion is what I dream,
A universe stuffed with unicorns, cats and colourful birds and whatever else I need.

A universe full of kind, loving people and enchanting animals,
On the way, you'll see birds chirping, talking cats and even fairies spreading sparkles.
As we walk on this eye-catching path, which will lead us to this enchanting paradise full of love.

Emilisa Qinami (9)
Oriel Academy West London, Hanworth

What Are Friends?

A friend is someone who is honest
Not someone who is dishonest
A friend is someone who cares
Not someone who is distrustful
A friend is someone who is as kind as a blossom
Not as rude and scary as a possum
Friends are as helpful as a mother or father
Not as horrifying and rude!

Amira Butt (9)
Oriel Academy West London, Hanworth

Harry Potter

H appiness of magic
O wls playing and delivering mail
G etting in the chamber
W ingardium Leviosa in the toilets
A t Hogsmeade
R acing to get the snitch
T he great Dumbledore has ruled for years.
S neaking out of bed.

Kacey Farinha (9)
Oriel Academy West London, Hanworth

Fantasy World

A land of fantasy is what we see,
An enchanting world awaiting me,
Bunnies, dragons, all these creatures in my head,
These images of pretend.
As Shakespeare said,
"Let there be gall enough in thy ink; though thou write with a goose-pen, no matter."

Liana Qinami (10)
Oriel Academy West London, Hanworth

A Wonderful Setting Of Wonderverse

A haiku

Stars guide young writers
Dreams glow in their crafted worlds
Wonderverse shines bright.

David Karl Morales (10)
Oriel Academy West London, Hanworth

The Unknown Yet To Be Discovered Secret Riddle

It's lovely and warming but sometimes dark and gloomy
Some are deadly and poisonous, others are sweet and beautiful
It's all around you, lurking wherever you seek
Be careful where you tread
Or you might fall into a trap (beautiful or ugly, it depends on the outcome)
So be aware and alert, do not let your guard down
It's watching and waiting, listening and calling
You might not realise it but it carries a dark, hideous and gloomy secret
What is it? you may wonder
Well, figure out the riddle to find the answer you so desperately seek.

Vanessa Kosciecha (10)
Park Lane Primary School, Whittlesey

Just Emotions

Joy is happy,
Sad is depressed,
Anger is raging,
Disgust is a mess,
But these are just emotions,
Joy has a toy,
Sadness has some badness,
Anger is a fighter,
Disgust likes stardust,
But all the same, they are just emotions.

Olivia Fitzjohn (10)
Park Lane Primary School, Whittlesey

Dreams

Dreams that are young
Dreams I'll hold forever
Dreams that I fight against
Dreams that burn
Dreams that grow
I'll still know.

Sophie Fitzjohn (10)
Park Lane Primary School, Whittlesey

There Are Four Seasons In A Year, And Each One Of Them Is Unique And Special!

Spring is a warm and cold season,
Spring is a time to celebrate life,
Spring is a great time to start afresh,
Spring makes me feel happy.

Summer is a time to see friends and family,
Summer is a time for adventure!
Summer is a wild season,
Summer makes me feel free.

Autumn is the season of pretty colours,
Autumn is the spooky season,
Autumn is a time to celebrate Halloween!
Autumn makes me feel like me.

Winter is the time to celebrate Christmas,
Winter is the season of a fresh start,
Winter is the time to celebrate love,
Winter makes me feel fresh.

Florence Mountain (10)
Penboyr Church In Wales Voluntary Aided Primary School, Llandysul

Going For Gold

O ars splashing
L egs running
Y achts speeding
M uscles working
P alms sweating
I nto the final
C yclists speeding
S uper athletes.

Millie Stanyer (7)
Pickhill CE Primary School, Thirsk

The Ferris Wheel That Led To Danger

We saw a plethora of rides
But me and my friend Olivia felt spontaneous
We saw a Ferris wheel, not any normal one
It was red and said, 'Death trap!'
We gave four tokens for the ride
I sat on the ride with Olivia
It started off at ten miles-per-hour, then to one hundred!
I felt sick, then all of a sudden, the man said, "It's broken!"
I screamed, "Argh!"
Then, all of a sudden, we landed on Mars
I was in shock!
I saw an alien in a UFO ship
Then I looked at my feet
They were floating off the ground
I screamed, but my voice just echoed
I cried and cried till I went back to Earth
I ran to hug Olivia and said, "We're never going on that again!"

Inara Daud (10)
Rawdhatul Uloom Primary School, Burnley

The Cave

In the cave, me and Dave were brave
In the dome was Nome, brushing his hair with a comb during a storm
There was a pitch, but it had a ditch and a witch who had a stitch
Dave was nauseous and I was cautious
I saw a bear that was ferocious
We had food that was stupendous
At the same looked meticulous
It was delicious
The water was nutritious
There was a fish that wanted a wish
Finally, in the town, there was a clown with a frown wearing a crown.

Izzadeen Hussain (9)
Rawdhatul Uloom Primary School, Burnley

Catch A Little Rhyme

Once upon a time,
I caught a little rhyme.

I set it on the floor,
But it ran right out the door.

I chased it on my bicycle,
But it melted to an icicle.

I scooped it up in my hat,
But it turned into a cat.

I caught it by the tail,
But it stretched into a whale.

I followed it in a boat,
But it changed into a goat.

When I fed it tin and paper,
It became a tall skyscraper!

Shihab Al Din (9)
Rawdhatul Uloom Primary School, Burnley

Clouds

Clouds are white and fluffy as candyfloss
And they love changing weather
When clouds feel down they cry
And when the sun comes with the rain
They work together to make a rainbow
Clouds are beautiful and precious
They are softer than anything in the world
And when it is night
They disappear into thin air only.

Rugaya Kabir (9)
Rawdhatul Uloom Primary School, Burnley

Winter

W inter is around the corner
I t's when everything freezes and turns to ice
N ot everyone hates winter
T here is lots of fun to be had
E njoying the beautiful snow
R olling in the snow is my favourite part.

Laseebah Raees (10)
Rawdhatul Uloom Primary School, Burnley

Animals Get Ready For Winter

A nimals get ready for winter.
U nderground, animals hibernate.
T he fall gets colder every day.
U seful people get stuff for winter.
M ummy makes hot chocolate for me.
N ights get longer.

Muhammed Khizar Khan (10)
Rawdhatul Uloom Primary School, Burnley

Nature Awakens

In the cradle of dawn where the soft whispers play,
Nature awakens in hues of gold and grey.
A tapestry woven of shadows and light,
Fields stretch like dreams beneath the first sight.

Forest trees tower, their arms stretched up high.
Guardians of stories, where echoes comply.
Leaves flutter beneath the boughs of ancient trees,
The meadows bloom with colours bright,
A canvas brushed in pure delight.

At dusk, the fireflies take their flight,
Painting shadows in golden light.
As twilight whispers soft and low,
The stars awaken one by one aglow.

In cycles of rhythm, in season's soft grace,
Nature whispers wisdom, we find our own space.
So let us remember in chaos or strife,
To tune into nature, the pulse of life.

Esther Adegoke (9)
Rosslyn Park Primary And Nursery School, Aspley

Shining Seasons

S oft petals bloom in gentle light,
P erfumed air, a sweet delight,
R adiant sun, a golden ring,
I n the air, songbirds sing,
N atures palette, colours bright,
G arnet skies in morning light.

S waying trees in the warm breeze,
U nfolding petals, buzzing bees,
M irthful laughter fills the air,
M ajestic sunset, colours fair,
E ager hearts, adventures aplenty,
R adient day, so free and plenty

W rapped in a cloak of icy white
I ntertwining branches glisten bright
N ature's canvas pure and cold
T ales of winter's beauty told
E ndless landscapes draped in snow
R evealing a quiet, tranquil show.

Mariama Lisse Kane (10)
Rosslyn Park Primary And Nursery School, Aspley

Be Wary Of Bad Friends!

Some friends can be our worst enemies
Some friends are often our foes
Some friends are better placed to plan our downfall
Some friends can be snakes
Some friends can be sell-outs
Our enemies at times prove to be our friends
Our enemies at times have our backs
Some friends become poisonous
Let's choose friends wisely
Let's take time in our selection
Lest we forget our choices
Lest we dread the day we met them
Let's choose our friends wisely
Many people are in jail because of bad friends
I don't know if you have heard this before
Evil friends' communications corrupt good manners
So if we are with evil friends
You could gradually see your good manners fly away.

Florence-Richard Okezie (10)
Rosslyn Park Primary And Nursery School, Aspley

Nature Is Getting Greater

I touch your face, I'm in your world
I have a lack of space and am beloved by birds
I am air, air is fair
We all care
We all know that the air is rare
Can run but never walk
Has a mouth and never talks
Has a bed and never sleeps
It's a river that is getting smarter
We all know that

Lava hates river
I wonder why
Nature is getting better and greater
You see it's full of wonder and destiny
But fire makes a choir
To destroy the atmosphere
So please donate money
So it can be sunny
That's why nature is greater.

Wealth Lazzerini (10)
Rosslyn Park Primary And Nursery School, Aspley

Tiger

I'm a tiger, stripy with fur.
Don't come here or I might growl.
Don't come here or I might growl.
Don't come here or I might bite.

Grace Adefarasin (9)
Rosslyn Park Primary And Nursery School, Aspley

Friendship

F un times
R eality doesn't exist
I n a world of our own
E lephants jump and dance
N othing can stop us
D oughnuts heal and help us
S unlight warms us
H oping it never ends
I magination supplying
P ictures keeping us alive.

Amelia Brearey (12)
Sir Frederick Gibberd College, Harlow

My Night Garden

Tiptoe, stay out of sight,
What little creatures can we hear tonight?

Snuffle, snuffle goes his little, black nose,
Cute and curious creep his tiny toes.
Suit of armour as sharp as thorns,
Searching for goodies on the lawns.

Tipetoe, stay out of sight,
What little creatures can we hear tonight?

A high-pitched cry and a sharp yapping bark,
Stalking, stealthily, leaving no mark.
A flash of red and a beacon of white,
As she creeps around in the deep, dark night.

Tiptoe, stay out of sight,
What little creatures can we hear tonight?

A piercing screech like a night alarm,
Before swooping and gliding, quiet and calm.
Her bright, wide eyes searching for prey,
Then retreating to her barn to snooze for the day.

Tiptoe, stay out of sight,
Let's sneak away now and whisper, "Goodnight."

Edie Snelle (7)
Spittal C.i.W. V.C. School, Spittal

All The Year's Parts

There are twelve parts to the year.
Start with January,
Most gorgeous of all.
Then go to February,
Happy Valentine's Day!
And you can't forget March,
It's pancakes, hooray!
April has its prime
As it comes to Easter morning,
Whilst May has its beauty,
But is kind of boring.
June makes you shiver
Like you're in the freezer.
As July makes rainbows across the crystal-clear skies,
August has its birthday parties in the night.
September has a gush of wind,
As October has a spooky night.
November has the Bonfire Night, alright!
Happy December!
It's time for the snow to come in,
And those are included in seasons,
Like red-coloured autumn,
Blank winter,

Yellow summer
And rainbow spring,
And finally, happy new year!

Maci Williams (9)
Spittal C.i.W. V.C. School, Spittal

Animals

A pes are big and swing all day.
N octurnal owls at night they play.
I nsects crawl on the jungle floor.
M agpies swoop to find shiny jewels and more.
A rctic foxes search below the snow.
L eopards so fast, watch them go.
S nakes slither silently out of sight. All these animals make the world right.

Elijah John (7)
Spittal C.i.W. V.C. School, Spittal

The Celts

C elts were fierce fighters, they fought like fearsome lions,
E very day the Celts fought ferociously like tigers in the wild,
L ots of them worked hard all day like a clock,
T hey also made sacrifices, as disgusting as a rat,
S o the Celts weren't very nice, like a terrible trench for a solemn soldier.

Thomas Bennet (7)
Spittal C.i.W. V.C. School, Spittal

Fresh Crisp Morning

As I opened my eyes there was a shiver down my spine
As I looked outside to the sunshine,
The grass sparkled bright,
Like the sunlight,
The leaves blew across the floor,
As the wind blew against the door,
As the birds sang their song,
The trees began to grow long.

Alfie Hawkins (8)
Spittal C.i.W. V.C. School, Spittal

My Friend And I

My friend and I.
She is tall and I am taller.
Her hair is long and mine is longer.
My friend and I.
She likes Pikachu and I like Cinnamoroll.
Her favourite colour is yellow and mine is purple.
My friend and I.
She swims like a dolphin and I ice skate like a penguin.
My friend and I live in different countries;
She is in Perth, Australia, and I am in Manchester.
My friend and I.
Though we are different, we love each other.
Hope our friendship will go deeper and deeper.

Tsz Tung Elizabeth Cheung (9)
St Alphonsus RC Primary School, Old Trafford

The Goblin Called Tall

The goblin called Tall
Is quite small,
He's rarely ever seen
And he's rude, green and mean,
He hides in the shadows,
He hears every step you take,
If you hear a rattle or shake,
You should run or hide
Before sunrise,
He's hungry
And angry!
If he sees you, run as fast as you can
Because he has a plan,
He wants blood on his hands.

Savannah Walker-Moore (10)
St Alphonsus RC Primary School, Old Trafford

I Know I Have A Friend

I know I have a friend because she sits at lunch with me
I know I have a friend because she loves me and hugs me

I know I have a friend because she makes me feel warm inside
I know I have a friend because she's always by my side

I know I have a friend because she's never mean to me
I know I have a friend because she sees what I could be

I know I have a friend because she makes me laugh out loud
I know I have a friend because she makes me proud.

Indie Brown (8)
St Andrew's CE (VA) Primary School, Fontmell Magna

Perspectives

Earth and Mercury spinning round,
Look closer, closer, closer, see
Something that may not have been.

Day or night, make sure you have good sight,
Because all the things you saw or heard could be different now.

Ever thought what the world would be
If all things were different to you and me?

So take time,
Look closer,
Notice more,
Because something might emerge
That you've never seen before.

Greta Briars (8)
St Andrew's CE (VA) Primary School, Fontmell Magna

Friendship Fun

Friends are important.
Happiness comes purely from friendships.
They are always helpful and kind.
They are truthful.
Truthful, they are always truthful.
Once or twice, they might possibly lie,
But friends are still friends till the very end.

Oscar Iles (8)
St Andrew's CE (VA) Primary School, Fontmell Magna

My Colourful Land Of Imagination

The colourful land of my imagination,
A land that comes from the corner of my mind,
The land with no descriptions,
This is my place,
A place filled with happiness and bliss,
It's my own land of fantasy,
Sometimes the land comes and goes,
And sometimes even flows.

If imagination was a game you could make,
I would probably bake it into a cake,
Oh, what fun it would be,
If I brought my friends with me,
For us to play and have an amazing day,
But then at night, in my dream so grand,
I'd go ride back to my Imagination Land.

Andrea Okodugha (9)
St Bernard's RC Primary School, Ellesmere Port

The Change Made By Us Humans

The birds flew and flew,
O'er green grasslands and sparkling seas,
O'er snow-covered mountains and forests full of life,
They caught fish in flowing rivers and worms on
The mysterious mountains for their dinner,
They drank water from the organic oceans.

The birds flew and flew,
O'er dead grasslands and contaminated seas,
O'er torrid mountains and rivers full of rubbish,
They caught rotten fish in polluted rivers and
Perished worms on the barren mountains
They drank brown water from the tainted oceans

Can you see the change made by us humans?

Aurora Chan (11)
St Catherine Of Siena RC Primary School, Lee Bank

Jocund Winter

J oy is here as winter is here
O verjoyed children laugh and play
C elestial skies, snow falls from
U ncountable snowflakes dancing in the whirling wind
N ostalgia you feel when the snow turns slushy
D ivine moments in this frosty season.

W himsical Winter, the director of shows
I ce cream icicles glisten tantalizingly
N ight skies are off the stage
T ranquillity is out, till spring hops in
E xquisiteness, evocativeness, make this a star performance
R oaring applause from the elated audience.

AJ Kabuta (9)
St Catherine Of Siena RC Primary School, Lee Bank

My Fairy Garden

The vibrant colours were spreading through the flowers
Through the flowers
The sun was proudly talking
About his energetic powers
The trees were dancing
The lovely creatures were prancing
The pretty fairies were flying
Through the air
The birds were looking after
Their little ones with care
The rivers were swaying
The dragons were slumbering
This is my fairy garden
So very beautiful
Where everyone is always cheerful
When I look at the glass dome from my bed
I wish I could be in it instead.

Michelle Rajan (9)
St Catherine Of Siena RC Primary School, Lee Bank

The Winter Night

A barn owl went to have a flight
Flying out then out of sight
A poor man was freezing cold
His thin dog was weak and old
A farmer's house was nearby
His house was warmer than outside
His goats were shivering at the side
He was generous but he was poor
He let the poor man get inside through the door
The pouring snow falling on the ground
Outside the house, there was no sound
Except for children who were playing in the snow
The snow was falling for some time, the time was very, very slow!

Andrew Poon (9)
St Catherine Of Siena RC Primary School, Lee Bank

Seasons, Seasons

Winter, winter in December,
All I can hear is the crunch-crunching of the snow,
And the snap-snapping of carrots.

Spring, spring in April,
All I can hear is the buzz-buzzing of the bees
And the chirp-chirping of the birds.

Summer, summer in August,
All I can hear is the splosh-sploshing of the tide,
And the click-clicking of crickets in the grass.

Autumn, autumn in September,
All I can hear is the whoosh-whooshing of the wind,
And the crunch-crunching of the leaves.

Saahiti Nagumalli (9)
St Catherine Of Siena RC Primary School, Lee Bank

Winter

Lonely leaves go as bare trees arise,
Children get excited when school ends.
Teachers leave but most stay with their sweet old classes.
Twenty-third of December has come and snowball fights begin.
It is as crazy as jumping off a hill.
Courageous children run as scared children hide.
The smell of hot chocolate fills the room.
All the children run home and enjoy.
Twenty-fifth of December children race to open their presents.
As snow slowly faints spring comes.

Eliana Asfaw (10)
St Catherine Of Siena RC Primary School, Lee Bank

What Is Friendship?

Friendship, friendship, what is friendship?
Friendship is like the sweetest candy in the world.
Friendship is like the shiniest star lighting the dark sky.
This star is even brighter than the sun.
Friendship is like the wonderful smell of roses.
Friendship is like the best thing of yours.
Friendship is like a bird singing.
A friendship is the best gift of all.

Letizia Lee (10)
St Catherine Of Siena RC Primary School, Lee Bank

Biting Cold Winter, Mild Autumn, Refreshing Spring And Sunlit Summer

In the chilling winter,
That bites you like a splinter,
Snow falls on the ground.
Here, spring is found,
All the flowers appear in the field,
A very refreshing season indeed!
Around the seasons go, here comes summer.
All the fun and music with the drummer,
And leaves that are as soft as cotton.
All the seasons pass so fast, here arrives autumn!
Red leaves that fall down
Onto the ground.

Angela Liu
St Catherine Of Siena RC Primary School, Lee Bank

A New Weird School

One day,
I arrived at school,
It looked similar,
But not quite normal.

Never had homework,
It never existed at this school!
"What is homework anyway?"
My school teacher said.

Never had there ever been,
A boring assembly at this school!
"Boring? That's a made-up word,"
The Deputy Head got confused at me.

Never had there been a school uniform!
"Unform is tight and annoying - wear what you like!"
The school office replied.

Never had a bully even stepped foot in this school!
"Surely you don't mean the animal - a bull?"
My friend said questionably.

And when I arrived at school on Friday,
You'll never guess what the headteacher said,
"School isn't on Fridays... What are you doing?"

Victoria Lowe (9)
St Catherine's Preparatory School, Bramley

Confused Teacher

Our teacher gave us extra homework when we were noisy.

Our teacher gave us extra homework when we did bad work.

Our teacher gave us no playtime when no homework was finished.

Our teacher gave us no playtime when we were messing around.

Then our headteacher said, "Your class are well-behaved, so if you want to keep your job please be kind."

After our headteacher said that, our teacher said we had to be naughty,

But not in other lessons - we behave perfectly!

Our confused teacher gets mad at us if we complete our homework.

Life is confusing, life is hard and life is different now we have a confused teacher

(Your homework is complete - that deserves detention!)

Madeleine Carlborg (9)
St Catherine's Preparatory School, Bramley

The Cat Who Loved Mats

Once, there was a cat,
Who loved sitting on mats,
All day long.
One morning, he found a drawing shaped like a paw.
He wondered what was there.
He thought, *this isn't fair.*
What was it? He didn't care.
So he jumped in. *Bang!*
The paw-shaped portal blew up,
And he nearly threw up!
Feeling weird, he kept on going for hours and hours.
For one moment, he felt like he had powers.
Zooming around from one side to the other,
Screaming, "I'm not like the others!"

Caitlin Irons (8)
St Catherine's Preparatory School, Bramley

The Universe

Have you ever imagined what the universe is like?
A big black cube or an enormous sphere?
Maybe you haven't thought about it,
Maybe just a bit.

The universe is endless!
Mostly dark and soundless.
We're not the only ones in space,
Who knows what there can be?

Galaxies and planets,
Scattered like dust.
Black holes and wormholes,
Somewhere out in space!

Have you ever imagined what the universe is like?
No one knows the whole story,
The universe is a mystery.

Hana Harding (9)
St Catherine's Preparatory School, Bramley

Chocolate

C hocolate is amazing!
H ow is it made? It is made from cocoa pods.
O rdinary chocolate is called milk chocolate.
C hocolate rating from me is 10/10!
O nly chocolate has its own twist and forever.
L oads of chocolates look the same, but they are all unique.
A ll types of chocolate have their own taste.
T here are all different types of chocolate: milk chocolate, white chocolate, dark chocolate.
E very chocolate is *delicious!*

Felicity McMorrow (8)
St Catherine's Preparatory School, Bramley

Winter

W inter is cold then *crack* goes the snow falling down with a smudge
I nside an igloo, it goes *crack* when you touch the wall
N ice sunny day shines on a lollipop, it melts and *crack*, it goes on the floor
T ake a red leaf then *crunch*, it broke
E aster bunny always gives you chocolate, then *crunch*, munch, you ate it all!
R attling in the breeze, leaves swirled around then *thud*, it landed on the ground.

Ines Wong (8)
St Catherine's Preparatory School, Bramley

In The Dog's Dog House

In the dog's dog house was a trophy,
In the trophy was a bone made of pure gold.
On the bone were letters saying, *Winner of Tug of War*.

The bone had a padlock,
So that no one could find out a code to a secret room,
The dog's owner did not know that there was a secret room.

In the room were pictures of dog friends
And trophies from tug-of-war games,
The dog went to when its owner was gone.

Alexis Chan (8)
St Catherine's Preparatory School, Bramley

Wonderful Seasons

Summer, winter, autumn, spring.
Every year the same,
They go round and round,
Just like a party game.

Summer, so hot,
Autumn, so twirly and fun,
Winter, as cold as ice in a bath,
Spring is full of daisies and life.

Summer brings crimson and roses,
Autumn brings rainbows and crunchy leaves,
Winter brings snowballs and hot chocolate,
Spring pervades the air with life.

Ariana Diaz (8)
St Catherine's Preparatory School, Bramley

I Am Jumping!

I am at the stables!
I get on Bounce, my horse
And we're off.
I am jumping high and low jumps.
I am jumping cross-bars and I trot over poles.
I am jumping with my horse
Bounce
So I am happy.
Suddenly, the judge says
"Well done"
And the crowd goes wild with approval.
A ten out of ten.
I did it
Again!

Beatrix Woodroffe (9)
St Catherine's Preparatory School, Bramley

Naughty Kittens

K ittens cuddling on the cosy couch
I ndigo, the invincible tabby, insists on instigating trouble
T omcat Thomas suddenly turns up at the teal door
T ime to take a walk to the tennis courts
E very evening at the eleventh hour
N ine naughty kittens not to be seen
S neaking silently under the starry skies.

Olivia Irvine (8)
St Catherine's Preparatory School, Bramley

Wonderland

W onderland could be anything
O ver the woods or on Pluto
N ever stop imagining
D are to be different
E nter the universe of your dreams
R ivers could be pink
L ike a flamingo
A nd express your feelings
N ot hide them
D reams and wonders you make, stored in Wonderland.

Katrina Tam (10)
St Catherine's Preparatory School, Bramley

The Wonders Of Seasons

Summer is quite hot,
Going to the beach is cool,
The pool is quite warm.

In autumn, leaves blow,
Autumn is very pretty,
September is cold!

December is nice,
Winter is not my favourite,
But I like Christmas!

Spring is beautiful!
Little lambs come out in spring!
Lush grass grows in spring.

India Dhew (9)
St Catherine's Preparatory School, Bramley

Winter

W inter is grey, with no life at all
I n the night, the creatures spring out, running and hunting all around
N estling birds cuddling their families
T rains pass, endlessly spreading their gas
E ver shining crystal ice glittering in the sun
R ain pouring down from the cloudy sky above.

Isabella Jones (8)
St Catherine's Preparatory School, Bramley

Dogman

D ogman is brave.
O rdinary Dogman is friendly and funny.
G o to the Dogman police station,
M eet the amazing Dogman.
A nimal to the crime, Dogman to the case.
N owhere to hide because Dogman will find you.

Zahra Bisi (9)
St Catherine's Preparatory School, Bramley

Myths And Monsters

In a land of the greatest core,
You can tell your friends what you saw,
You can so definitely do that,
Or go back to find a Calydonian boar.
Hobbits always have their thirds,
In a land of beasts and birds,
Not many of them are nerds.
But some have probably heard,
Of a carnivorous cow and a hawk with a towel.
At this you would bow but you would soon say how,
Because this sort of air makes you float like a dare,
A dragon, like a bear with a flair who needs lots of care
On his wings as he flies overhead like the sky's new king,
This meta Mina can cause a gigantic crash,
Helped by a pig with a purple dash.
The herbivorous scorpions cash were a cousin of the Nash
But the size and scale at least,
The Nomunavaa is the size of a car and would never
Pay for the bar but couldn't even walk so far
Unlike the Factotoa, the Xiocarr and the X-ray dhaa who usually lives in taa.

Rafe Jubber (9)
St George's CE Primary School, Langton Matravers

Surfing Waves

The ocean is vast; crashing waves, swirling water.
I'm scared and excited at the same time.
I say to myself I've got this.
I start to paddle and stand up on my surfboard.
I glide down the wave.
It makes me feel like I want to scream and shout.
I get this lovely feeling that my Mum and Dad are cheering me on.
I paddle back out for another one.

Elowen Hoad (7)
St George's CE Primary School, Langton Matravers

Autumn, Winter, Summer

Crunch... crunch... crunch...
The cloud-like snow dissolves at your touch
Crunch... crunch... crunch...
Small snowflakes fall and numb your face
But you stay discrete
Crunch... crunch... crunch...

Snap, snap, snap
Warm-toned leaves seem ostentatious in your eyes
And warmth travels up your spine
Snap, snap, snap
Twigs break beneath you.

Splash, splash, splash
Children play in the pool around you
Splash, splash, splash
The beaming sun shines on your back
And you slowly fall into a dreamless sleep.

Isabella Wood (9)
St Gerard's RC Primary School, Castle Vale

St Gilbert's Super Space Expedition

S oar through the twinkling sky of planets,
P oor Neptune needs some blankets,
A liens pulling at Neil A's arm,
C ourse they don't mean any harm,
E arth was my home but now the moon is my superdome...

Robyn Bland (10)
St Gilbert's RC Primary School, Winton

Monsters Everywhere

Monsters come beneath the stones,
Sometimes you see them eating bones.
In the shadows,
Always hiding from daylight,
Waiting for a moment to jump out and make a fright.

Monsters here, monsters there,
Luckily, they aren't everywhere.
Open my eye and all is okay,
Monsters aren't real, hip hip hooray!

Lily Hammond (8)
St John The Baptist CE (C) Primary School, Waltham Chase

Halloween

On Halloween night,
Carved pumpkins are a sight,
The decorations might make you shiver,
The haunted house will make you quiver,
At midnight, curses do occur,
Have monsters with matted fur,
Trick-or-treating is a pleasure,
But most costumes are made of leather.

Scarlett Blake (8)
St John The Baptist CE (C) Primary School, Waltham Chase

Divine

Oh, sweet Divine,
Forever mine,
It glows in the heart,
Which shows a glorious piece of art.

Divine, which is flown in the air,
Never a wail of despair,
Happy kids dancing in the sun,
No trouble, but just having fun.

Peaceful birds playing tunes,
It's so beautiful,
Makes me feel I am in the month of June,
I wish I could hear them more, maybe soon.

I look up to the heavenly sky,
I see the wonders and it's so high,
Also, the colours of the rainbow,
Watching all the colours grow and flourish.

Nicole Chizitere Eke (10)
St Peter's Catholic Primary School, Dagenham

A Beautiful Day

It's such a beautiful day,
I guess it's time to go outside and play,
I feel so nice,
Also, I played games and won twice.

The sun is shining bright,
It's like I'm surrounded with just light.
Sadly, we have to go because of time,
But at least I brought my favourite slime.

Alex Chima Eke (7)
St Peter's Catholic Primary School, Dagenham

My Friend And Me

My friends make the world go round
We really like to play around
We are best of friends forever
And we will become so clever
We sing together and dance together
And all of our friends play together
We all like Stitch
And we play football
I have a friend
Who likes to spend
Time with me
In the sea.

Sophie Ledbrooke (8)
St Stephen Churchtown Academy, St. Austell

My Magical Box

Inspired by The Magic Box by Kit Wright

I've got a magical box,
And anything can go in it like a dog or a slide,
So let's find out what I can put inside,
I could put a star from space
Or a warm embrace,
I could put a really big house
Or a tiny little mouse,
I could put a cheerful dog
Or a very long log,
I could put a huge whale
Or a small, slow snail,
I could put a wooden boat
Or a wonderful quote,
I could put a spooky ghost
Or a very mean roast,
I could put an extremely strong bull
And now my magical box is full
And that is the end of my poem.

Abdul Hannan (10)
Stoke Minster CE Primary Academy, Stoke-On-Trent

A Beautiful Sunday

Blessed are we with the Earth
Ingrained in it is the gift of life
A gift we have is time
Time of the centuries
I love this one day of the week
Full of jubilation and prayer
Understanding is like holding an atom
Listen to the birds as they sing
Some go to church and pray
Underestimating it would be a lapse
Nobody stays at home but instead takes a break
Dandelion seeds get dispersed with wishes
As silent as the night, the river flows
You may hear crickets sing their song.

Charis Antiaye (10)
The Blessed Sacrament Catholic Primary School, Ribbleton

Serene Seasons

Spring:
Spring is when all the animals come out
In spring when you are growing you might see a little sprout

Summer:
Summer is hot like porridge when it's out of the pot
In summer nothing will rot because it is lovely and hot

Autumn:
Autumn is cool as the leaves change colour in town
When they are brown they start to fall down

Winter:
Winter is cold, it's known for snow
As snowdrops start growing they might be as small as your pinky toe!

Charlene Charley (8)
The Marton Academy, Marton

The Cat And The Lion

The cat was walking in the forest when he saw a lion on a mat, sleeping. So, the cat walked back a bit. Then he stepped on a stick and woke up the lion. Then he ran away. Just then, the lion ran after it. The cat got to a dead end and the lion picked him up in his mouth and took him to his secret home that none of the other animals could find.

Just then, the lion roared as loud as he could, but then he lost his roar and this made him very sad. He started to cry.

The mouse said, "Don't cry. I can help you."

The lion said, "Really?"

The mouse said, "Yeah."

The mouse gave him some medicine and the lion got his roar back. The lion thanked the mouse.

"Do you want to be friends?" asked the mouse.

"Yes," said the lion.

Serenity Gracie-Mai Irwin (8)
The Merton Primary School, Leicester

He's Back Again!

The big black spider is back again,
He has black skin and hairy legs,
He's got blue eyes like the sky.
"How colourful they are," said Mrs Swan,
"Why thank you, they are as blue as the sky."
I have to say, swinging side to side,
On his web, it feels like sloppy bread.
When I see him near my bed,
I think he'll come out by my head.

That big fat spider is back again
No one likes him, what a shame.
He's big and fat and acts like a bat.
I count eight eyes and I count eight legs,
But I only ever count just the one head.
He crawls really slowly and then really fast,
You should see him jump, over the grass.
He finds a corner to go to sleep,
You don't hear a thing, not even a peep.

Skyla Stretton (8)
The Merton Primary School, Leicester

Autumn Treasure Hunt!

1, 2, 3, throw a stick up in the chestnut tree.

4, 5, 6, gold falls from a twig.

7, 8, 9, nature's treasures for all to find.

Some in prickly cases,

Some smooth on the ground,

Some to make crafts,

Some to scare away the spiders,

The bigger the better,

The smoother the shinier,

Fun to find for old and young,

Conkers, autumn's natural treasure hunt!

Quinn Evelyn Goff (9)
The Merton Primary School, Leicester

Will You Be My Friend?

Sitting all alone on her first day of school
Her heart as hard as a brick
Feeling scared and sad
Her blood as frozen as ice
Standing alone
Is there anyone to help her?
Or anyone to talk to?
She says to herself, "Will I find a friend?"
Then she looks up and sees someone smiling
She feels a glow in her heart and asks,
"Will you be my friend?"

Riya Patel (8)
The Merton Primary School, Leicester

The Unknown Blackness

Space with its endless mass of blackness of terror.
Yet it remains the most beautiful mystery of them all.
History began with the Big Bang,
Scattering its infinite worlds of stars, planets, and galaxies like grains of sand.
Magical adventure towards the unknown is waiting to be explored.
Planets of icy, frozen, moving water,
Fiery, flaming and flowing fire,
Of constant and everchanging hostility, home that we call Terra.
Somewhere in the outer space, there is a dwarf star.
Shining, shimmering and sparkling so bright.
Like a gentle glimmer in a child's eye,
Somewhere in outer space, there is a dying star.
Exhausted and collapsing into itself, into an endless black hole.
Like a decaying flower at its first taste of autumn.
Billions, billions and billions of miles away. From the unknown and rampant space,
Safe in my little room with a pen, I watch in awe and constant glee.
As the mysterious space is unravelled, one by one.
That I no longer fear its blackness.

Nevaeh Asongo-Cassell (10)
The Ridgeway Primary School, Reading

Flying Seasons

Every year the seasons fly
Summer floats up in the sky
People swimming and shouting with glee
Children playing as free as a bee.

In winter people choose to stay inside
Drinking hot chocolate with pride
Sitting near fires, trying to stay warm
When it's cold the wind might form a storm.

When it's spring the flowers bloom
Very soon disappears all the gloom
Bright smiles on every face
This season's for anyone no matter what race.

In autumn the leaves can die
When it is Thanksgiving family visit by
Twigs tumbling to the ground
I love this autumn that I've found.

Ayra Mohamed Ashif (9)
The Ridgeway Primary School, Reading

Space Wonders

Sometimes I wish space had an end,
But when anyone adventures there,
Someone always needs a mend.

Pluto's a planet that everyone hates,
He's just a planet stuck in space.
The sun is very hot,
Hotter than a steaming hotpot.

Sometimes I wonder how stars were invented,
Sometimes I think that the stars are scented,
Could be lemon, apple or orange,
The wildest one of all could be porridge!

Space is wonderful for you to see,
The moon and sea are one to be,
From the stars to the coral reef.
The best part of space,
Is that there's a place called Space Wonders!

Phoebe Nunn (9)
The Ridgeway Primary School, Reading

Who Is She?

My name is Evelyn and I am nine.
Can you guess this best friend of mine?
July 28th, the best day yet.
That was the day she and I met.
She taught me how to crawl and walk.
She even helped me learn to talk.
My first word was Dad but he isn't she,
Who do you think she could be?
Her smile shines bright like the sun,
We laugh, we play and have lots of fun.
I love her most, she is the best,
Are you able to make a guess?
Her name is Jemma, she is 31.
My best friend and my mum.
I am me and she is she.
Without her I would be me.

Evelyn Carroll (9)
The Ridgeway Primary School, Reading

The Dancing Seasons

Autumn is the sunset season
Leaves fall from the trees
You hear crunches in every step
You see the colours pink, orange and gold.

Winter is the time of ice
Cold, damp, frosty
The leaves on the trees are lost
Always snowing, raining, hailing.

Spring is when the flowers are blooming
Grass the greenest green
Flowers so vibrant, colourful
Sky the bluest blue.

Summer is the season of the sun
Trees with all their leaves
Flowers with all their petals
A time to relax.

Katelin Krasniqi (9)
The Ridgeway Primary School, Reading

What Is?

What is red?
A rose is red, waiting to curl up into its cosy bed.

What is orange?
The sun is orange, waiting for its morning porridge.

What is yellow?
A sunflower is yellow, waiting for its first ever 'marshmellow'.

What is green?
The grass is green, hoping the sunflowers wouldn't be so mean.

What is blue?
The sky is blue, hoping the birds would soon fly through.

What is violet?
Flowers are violet, hoping that they'll soon find their pilot.

Evie Hewett (9)
The Ridgeway Primary School, Reading

Off To War

Underground, but not waiting for a train
Ears ringing from the siren's sound
A loud *thud* hits the ground
Later we surface to the sound of pain.

All the boats line up on the shore
Run on the beach and find some cover
Was the last sound I heard from another wave
Of the sea, a red never seen before.

For how long must we stay on this bridge
Tales from home in a letter
Makes for five minutes better
While hoping tigers are not over the ridge.

William Robinson (9)
The Ridgeway Primary School, Reading

The Four Seasons

There are four different seasons but only one year
When one season finishes a new one will appear

Every time in spring, flowers start to grow
Wait for about two months and summer says hello

Summer is when the trees grow tall
Autumn is when leaves start to fall

Winter comes the final season of the year
And then again spring will appear

That's the four seasons in only one year
Everyone knowing that spring is near.

Levi Potter (9)
The Ridgeway Primary School, Reading

The Autumn Season

October is to be remembered,
It's when you seek the days of autumn,
The leaves change colour,
And fall apart.

It starts to rain and rain and rain,
And also gets very cold,
It starts to get so soggy,
And plants start to die.

It gets colder and colder,
You might even get frostbite,
So you better be careful,
Winter is sneaking in.

Yomola Erinoso (9)
The Ridgeway Primary School, Reading

As Summer Goes By

As summer goes by,
My skin is red.
Splash in pools,
Using all the tools.

The sea is nice and calm,
Much better than being on a farm.
Lemonade on the beach,
My skin turning peach.

As the wind blows and the summer goes,
As the waves might be a bit rough,
You will think of the lovely things you have done,
As summer goes by.

Izabela Banas (9)
The Ridgeway Primary School, Reading

Rising Of Spring

'Out of the cave, out of the hole,
Bear, rabbit and a little mole'.
The leaves are turning green and snow already melted.
The flowers green, pink and blue sway in happiness.

As the sun gets warmer birds tweet,
A perfect creation of knitted lines,
Hanging from tree to tree.
Spiders crawl catching a fly as another night falls.

Latoya Ndlovu (9)
The Ridgeway Primary School, Reading

The Blueberry Wish List

Let me be sweet like a sugar cube,
Let me be tart like a delicious pie,
Let me be the best of the cluster on the shrubby bush,
Let me be deep indigo like the night sky,
Let me be firm, but not overly soggy,
Let be more popular than my red friends the cranberries,
And please, please do not let me be eaten by the slender, sneaky squirrels.

Isla Snarey (9)
The Ridgeway Primary School, Reading

The Super Sunny Summer

Summer is gone, that's such a bummer
If only winter was like summer
Summer is a ray of sunshine
Sunshine is bright, unlike a dead vine.

Summer holidays, no more school
No more homework, that's the greatest rule
Winter's chilly, gives flu and colds
Try to be strong, try to be bold.

Jewel Awhana (9)
The Ridgeway Primary School, Reading

The Magical World Out There

Beyond the night sky, where aliens might fly,
In a magical place, known as space.
Starting my rocket, off I go,
Passing mysterious places, I may not know.
On Mars, there are a lot of stars
That all look like tiny cars.
This is really a wonderful place,
But now it's time to say bye to space.

Eli Murphy (9)
The Ridgeway Primary School, Reading

Animals In The Amazon

Cheeky monkeys swing on trees all day,
As sleepy sloths snore all night.
Dangerous cheetahs hunting for their prey,
Silent capybaras soaking in the river.
Black bats flying back home before sunrise,
This is the wonderful life in the Amazon Rainforest.

Calista Kwan (9)
The Ridgeway Primary School, Reading

Mother Nature

The world is crying,
The Earth is dying.
Think about the future,
And care about nature.

Keep the earth clean,
Please don't be mean.
Solution to keep our world tidy,
There's a variety,
Don't be cruel to the society.

Samaira Sharma (9)
The Ridgeway Primary School, Reading

The New Girl

The girl that's new,
Is better than you.
I tried to reach her,
But she's always ahead.
I felt better with arts,
But she got me at maths,
And when I decided to challenge at ski,
I figured out that she was just me.

Hiyori Minakawa (8)
The White House Preparatory School, London

Nature, Beautiful Nature

N othing as wonderful as nature, squirrels jumping from tree to tree, bees buzzing from flower to flower and a robin dancing from bush to bush
A mazing insects busily searching for food
T ime stands still as the autumn leaves fall
U nder the great blue sky, watch the clouds float gracefully by
R ays of sunshine waking up the drowsy flowers
E ach day something extraordinary happens, wonderful for us all to enjoy.

Logan Taylor (8)
Willow Green Academy, Ferrybridge

Don't Give Up

I can't do this – yet
I don't understand – yet
It doesn't work – yet
But
I bet
If I tried
I wouldn't cry
And with my family by my side
I can do anything with pride
So what I'm trying to say is

Don't give up!

Molly Bishop (10)
Wycliffe CE Primary School, Shipley

YOUNG WRITERS INFORMATION

We hope you have enjoyed reading this book – and that you will continue to in the coming years.

If you're the parent or family member of an enthusiastic poet or story writer, do visit our website **www.youngwriters.co.uk/subscribe** and sign up to receive news, competitions, writing challenges and tips, activities and much, much more! There's lots to keep budding writers motivated!

If you would like to order further copies of this book, or any of our other titles, then please give us a call or order via your online account.

Young Writers
Remus House
Coltsfoot Drive
Peterborough
PE2 9BF
(01733) 890066
info@youngwriters.co.uk

Join in the conversation!
Tips, news, giveaways and much more!

YoungWritersUK   YoungWritersCW

youngwriterscw   youngwriterscw